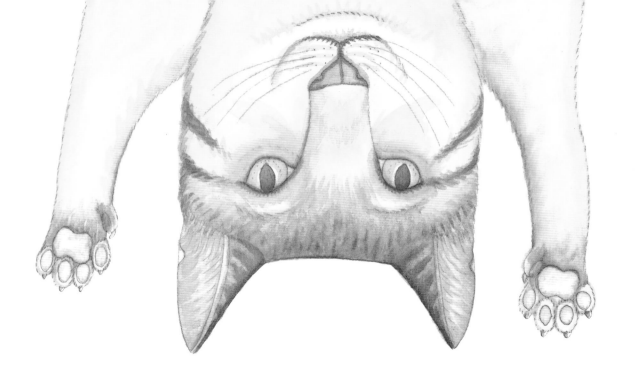

Raining
Cats and
Dogs

Written by **JANE YOLEN**

Illustrated by **JANET STREET**

HARCOURT BRACE & COMPANY

San Diego   New York   London

Requests for permission to make copies of any part of the
work should be mailed to: Permissions Department,
Harcourt Brace & Company, 8th Floor,
Orlando, Florida 32887.

"Hunting Song" first appeared in *Cricket*, November 1976,
volume 4, number 3.
"To My Puppy" first appeared under the title "A Valentine to
My Puppy" in *Cricket*, February 1992, volume 19, number 6.
"Mother Cat's Purr" first appeared in *Dragon Night and
Other Lullabies*, published by Methuen, 1981.

Library of Congress Cataloging-in-Publication Data
Yolen, Jane.
Raining cats and dogs/by Jane Yolen; illustrated
by Janet Street. — 1st ed.
p.   cm.
Summary: A collection of nine poems about cats and nine
poems about dogs, bound together in an upside-down book.
ISBN 0-15-265488-7
1. Cats—Juvenile poetry.   2. Dogs—Juvenile poetry.
3. Children's poetry, American.   [1. Cats—Poetry.   2. Dogs—
Poetry.   3. American poetry.]   I. Street, Janet, ill.   II. Title.
PS3575.043R45   1993
811'.54—dc20   91-24295

Printed in Singapore

First edition

A B C D E

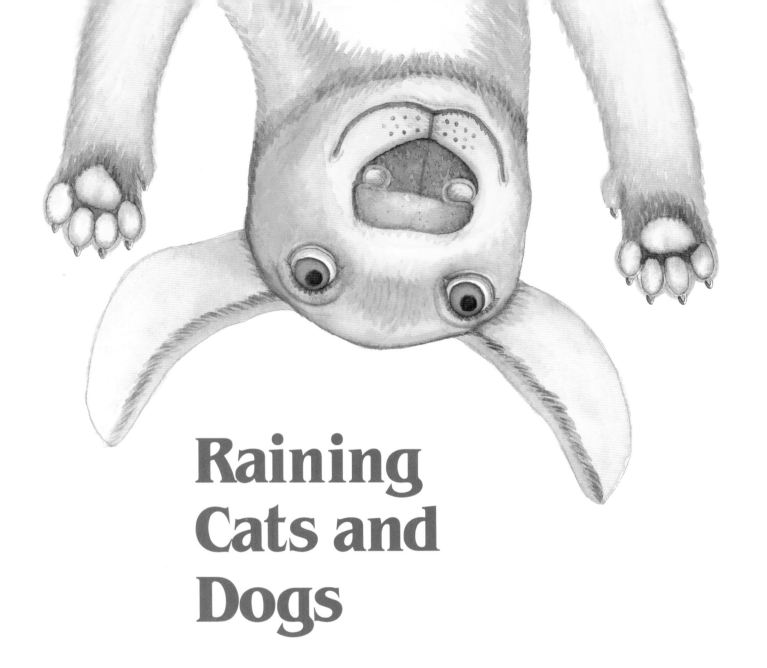

Raining Cats and Dogs

Written by **JANE YOLEN**

Illustrated by **JANET STREET**

HARCOURT BRACE & COMPANY

San Diego   New York   London

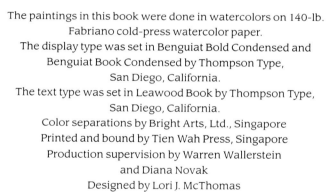

The paintings in this book were done in watercolors on 140-lb.
Fabriano cold-press watercolor paper.
The display type was set in Benguiat Bold Condensed and
Benguiat Book Condensed by Thompson Type,
San Diego, California.
The text type was set in Leawood Book by Thompson Type,
San Diego, California.
Color separations by Bright Arts, Ltd., Singapore
Printed and bound by Tien Wah Press, Singapore
Production supervision by Warren Wallerstein
and Diana Novak
Designed by Lori J. McThomas

To Tim Peck,
even though he is a horse person

—*J. Y.*

I AM CAT

I am silk and velvet,
I am spit and squall,
I am stretch of moonlight,
I am river's crawl,
I am motor purring,
I am slit of eye,
I am whispers running,
I am . . .
       I.

I am creep of claw clicks,
I am corduroy tongue,
I am green lights winking,
I am screaming sung,
I am sand on bare skin,
I am water dry,
I am whispers landing,
I am . . .
       I.

ALLEY CAT SPEAKS

I'm an alley cat,
  an oily cat,
  an only cat,
    a hermit.

Show me one trick
  or one trunk
  or one can —
    I'll learn it.

I can open any,
  exit any,
  enter any
    door.

I can steal a little,
  stretch a little,
  stalk a little
    more

Than your ordinary,
  every dairy,
  any wary
    cat.

And there's not a butcher's
  baker's
  farmer's pet
    who can say that!

WHAT IS A KITTEN?

What is a kitten?
It's tail chase and pounce.
It's skittering claws and
A stop with a bounce.

What is a kitten?
It's milky blue eyes
That close into slots
And then moon in surprise.

What is a kitten?
It's ear-squeaking mew
That sounds like an oiling
Is long overdue.

What is a kitten?
It's thistledown fur.
It's curl in a cupboard.
It's purrrrrrrrrrrrrrrr.

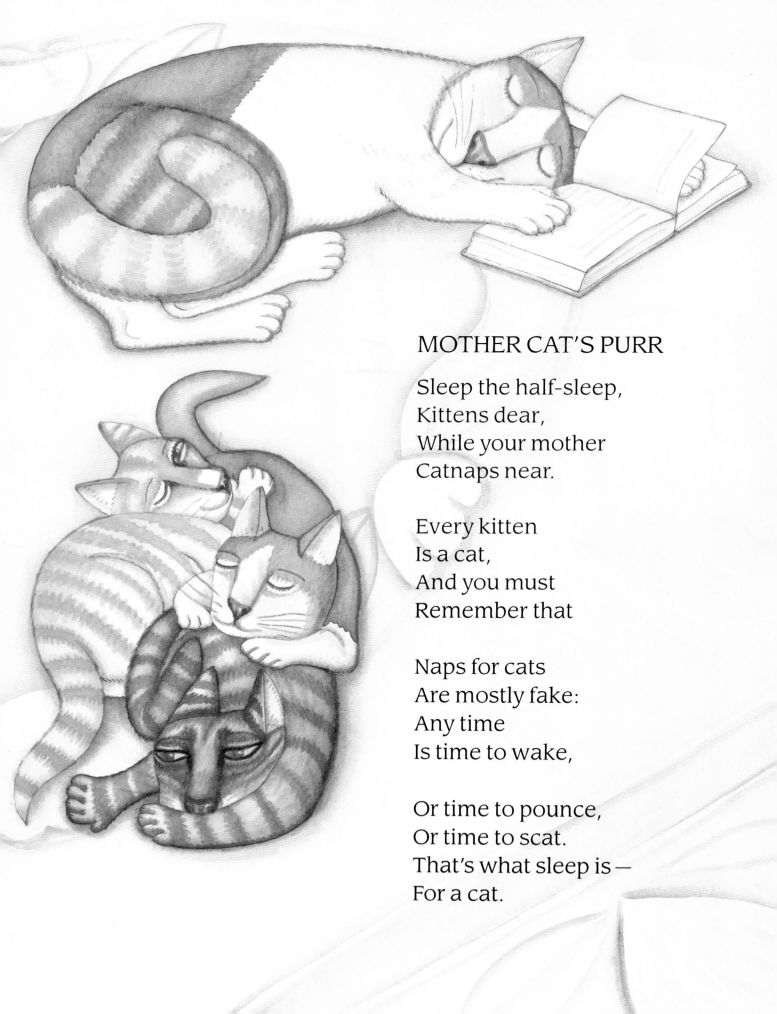

MOTHER CAT'S PURR

Sleep the half-sleep,
Kittens dear,
While your mother
Catnaps near.

Every kitten
Is a cat,
And you must
Remember that

Naps for cats
Are mostly fake:
Any time
Is time to wake,

Or time to pounce,
Or time to scat.
That's what sleep is —
For a cat.

NIGHT HOWLS

Outside the house,
The night's all howls,
With cat paw creeps
And cat claw prowls,

And the little *swish-swash*
Of a cat conclave
That howls to life
The dead down grave.

If the door be open,
If the window wide,
I will leap lap over
And land outside

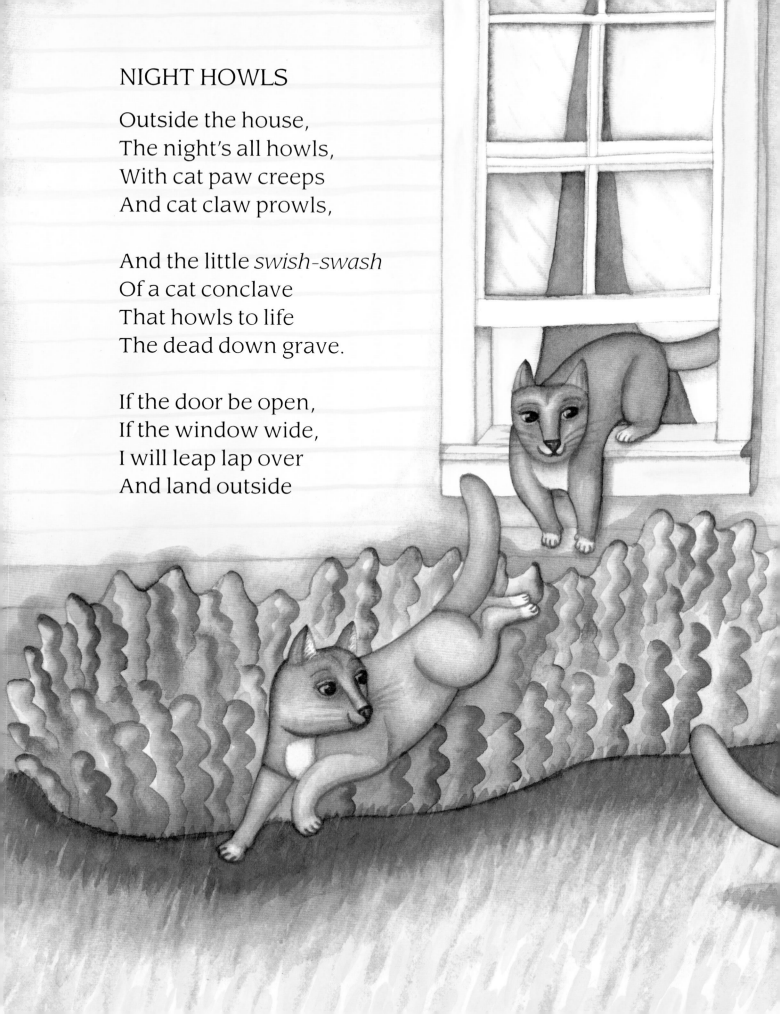

To raise my yowl
To the mindless moon,
A heaven-long howl
Not quite in tune.

If the door be closed,
And the window, too,
I will lap my leg
From dirt to new,

I will show disdain
For the late howl night,
I will coil in a curl
Beneath the light.
                    Good night.

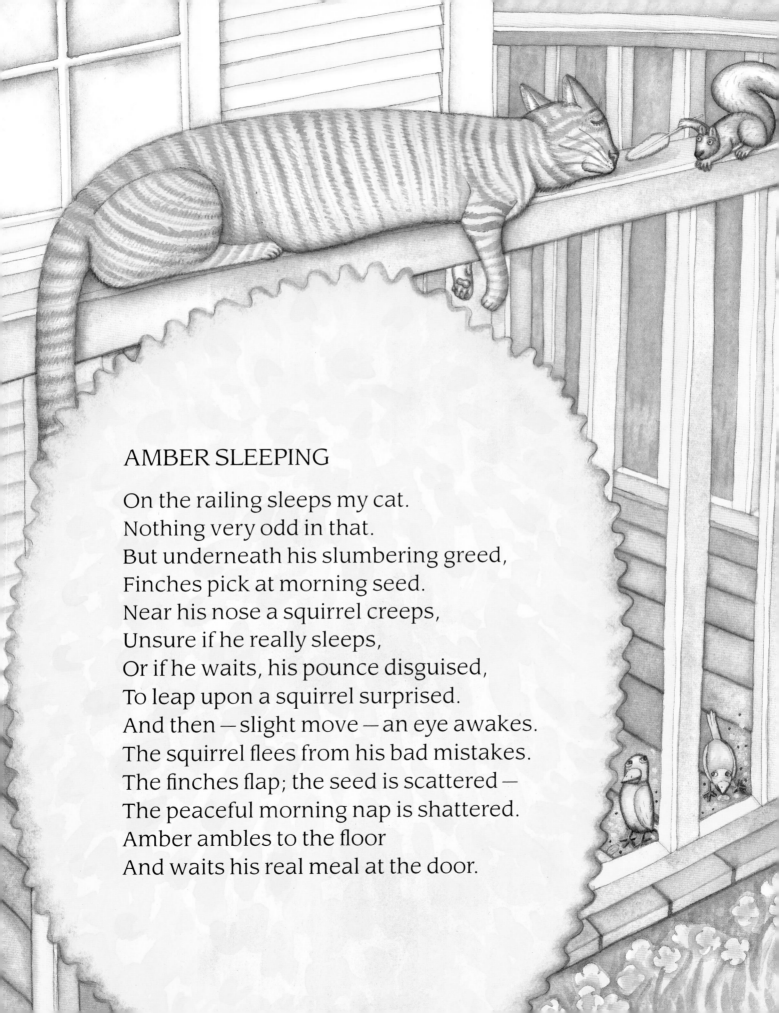

AMBER SLEEPING

On the railing sleeps my cat.
Nothing very odd in that.
But underneath his slumbering greed,
Finches pick at morning seed.
Near his nose a squirrel creeps,
Unsure if he really sleeps,
Or if he waits, his pounce disguised,
To leap upon a squirrel surprised.
And then — slight move — an eye awakes.
The squirrel flees from his bad mistakes.
The finches flap; the seed is scattered —
The peaceful morning nap is shattered.
Amber ambles to the floor
And waits his real meal at the door.

STALKING

A tremble of grass
as I pass.

A shadow of claws
as I pause.

A whisper of feet
as I leap.

And the crunching of bones
after.

OLD SOOT

His fur is black; we call him Soot,
But underneath his chin
Some little hairs of gray and white
Have started to come in.

He sometimes stalks out in the fields
Or fishes in our streams,
But mostly what he catches now
Are in his catnap dreams.

He watches shadows cross the floor
And with a lazy paw
Will reach to touch one if it's close
Or snag it with his claw.

But mostly he just sits and licks
Himself from head to toe
So he will be presentable
When it is time to go.

RAINING CATS

It's raining cats,
A cataract,
A waterfall,
With felines stacked.
One, two, and three —
Catastrophe,
They're purring down
On top of me.

RAINING DOGS

It's raining dogs,
A doggone shame,
This flood has only
Hounds to blame.
Dogmatically,
They're splashing down,
And cur-rents cover
Half the town.

Some dogs shed,
And some are shaved.
Some are savers,
Some are saved.
Some are bought
In high-class shops.
Some work farms,
Some work with cops.
Some dogs howl,
And some do not.
(And some dogs yip
And yap a lot!)

Some dogs leap,
And some dogs slog.
Some dogs trot,
And some dogs jog.
Some dogs sleep off
Half the day;
Some dogs always
Want to play.
But best of all
The dogs to get
Is my dog—'cause
He's sure *some* pet!

SOME DOGS

Some dogs guard,
And some dogs guide.
Some dogs find you,
Some dogs hide.
Some dogs hunt,
And some dogs herd.
Some come to whistles,
Some to a word.
(And some do not
Come when you call
But, ostentatious,
Play at ball!)

Some dogs growl,
And some dogs bite.
Raise a stick,
And some take flight.
Some dogs wait
Until you fling
Away the stick,
Then bring the thing
Back to your feet,
A doggy game.
(For some dogs have
So little shame!)

DOG DREAMS

A scrabble of nail
Upon hearthstone,
A deep-throated whine,
And then he's gone,

Coursing the dream lanes,
Over the moor,
Chasing the red squirrel,
Chasing the hare.

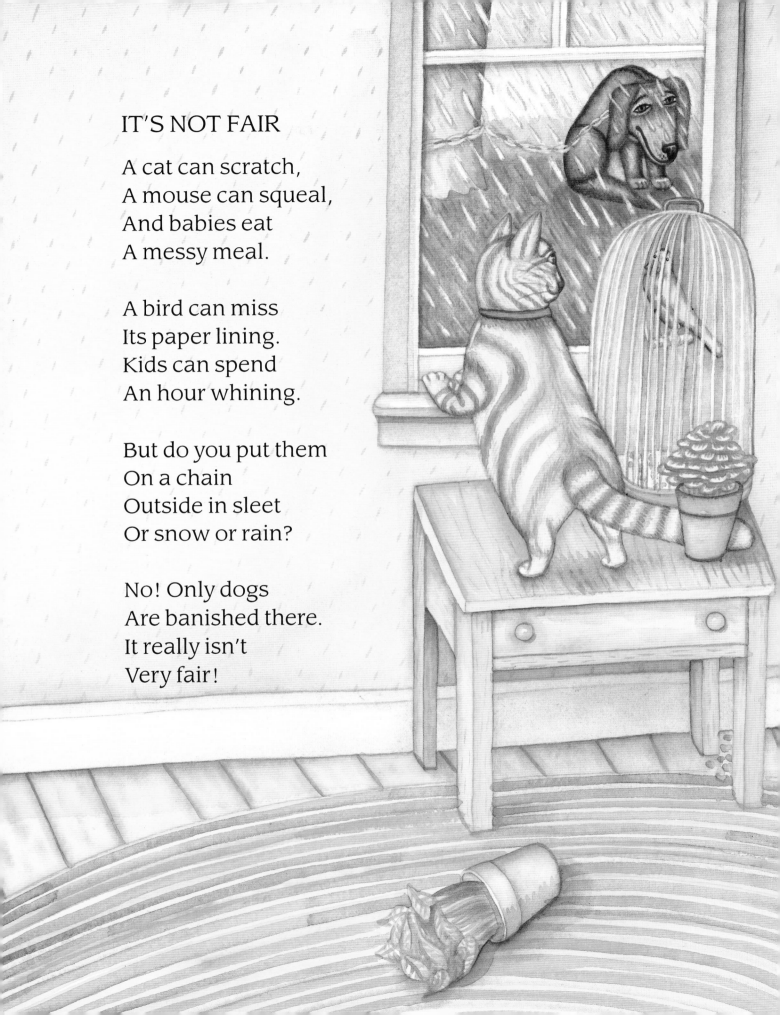

IT'S NOT FAIR

A cat can scratch,
A mouse can squeal,
And babies eat
A messy meal.

A bird can miss
Its paper lining.
Kids can spend
An hour whining.

But do you put them
On a chain
Outside in sleet
Or snow or rain?

No! Only dogs
Are banished there.
It really isn't
Very fair!

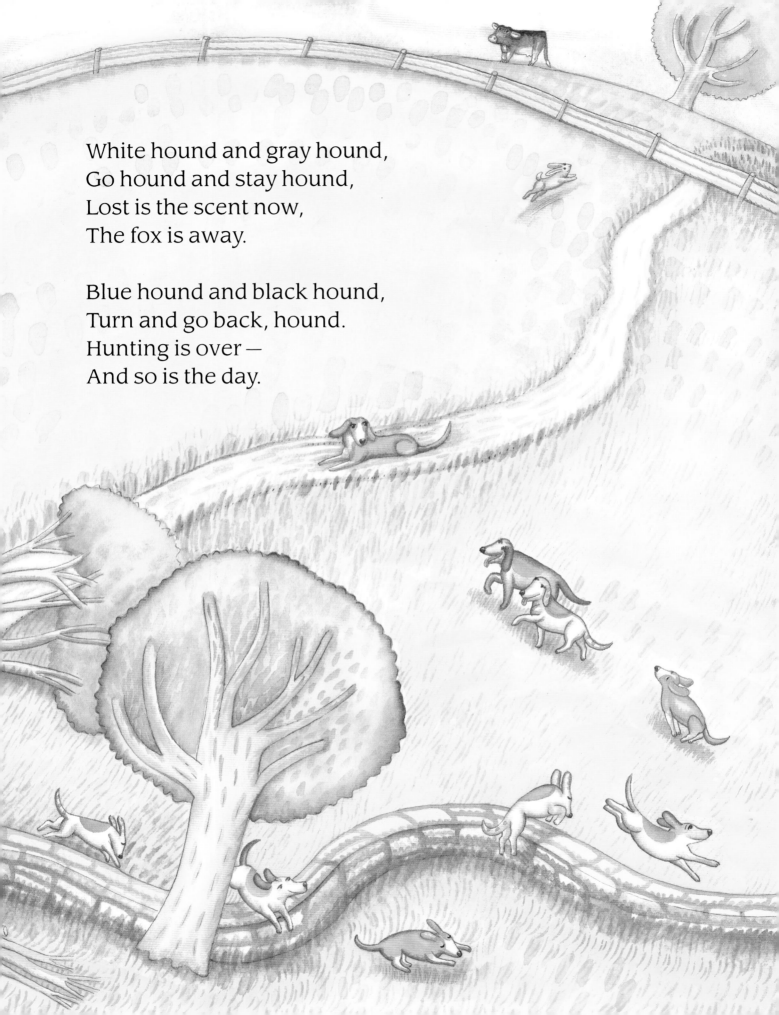

White hound and gray hound,
Go hound and stay hound,
Lost is the scent now,
The fox is away.

Blue hound and black hound,
Turn and go back, hound.
Hunting is over —
And so is the day.

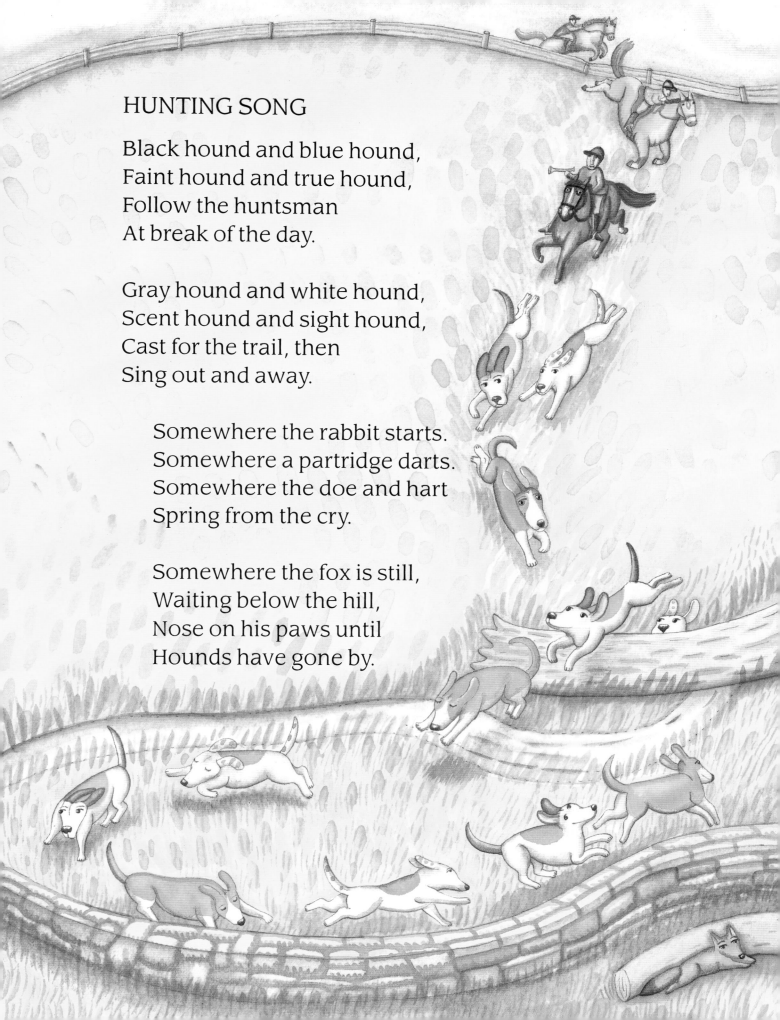

HUNTING SONG

Black hound and blue hound,
Faint hound and true hound,
Follow the huntsman
At break of the day.

Gray hound and white hound,
Scent hound and sight hound,
Cast for the trail, then
Sing out and away.

Somewhere the rabbit starts.
Somewhere a partridge darts.
Somewhere the doe and hart
Spring from the cry.

Somewhere the fox is still,
Waiting below the hill,
Nose on his paws until
Hounds have gone by.

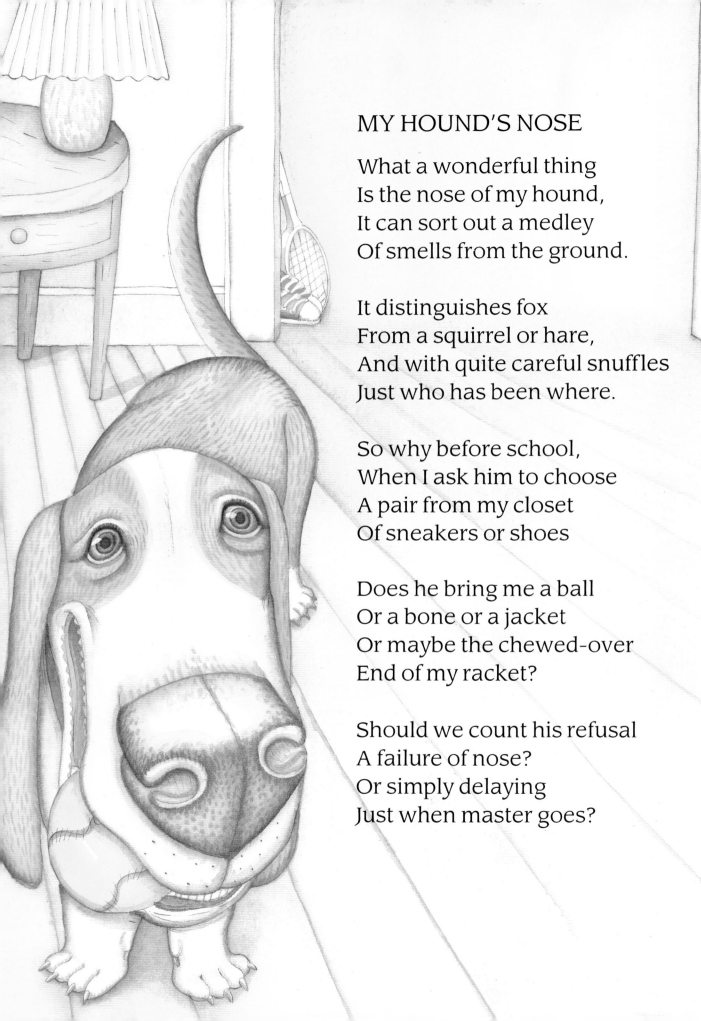

MY HOUND'S NOSE

What a wonderful thing
Is the nose of my hound,
It can sort out a medley
Of smells from the ground.

It distinguishes fox
From a squirrel or hare,
And with quite careful snuffles
Just who has been where.

So why before school,
When I ask him to choose
A pair from my closet
Of sneakers or shoes

Does he bring me a ball
Or a bone or a jacket
Or maybe the chewed-over
End of my racket?

Should we count his refusal
A failure of nose?
Or simply delaying
Just when master goes?

TO MY PUPPY

I think of you, I think of bones,
The tooth-marked cords of telephones,
The loose ends of upholstered chairs,
A slipper with the heel in tears,
A rubber ball, a mangled sock,
The splintered mass of baby's block.
These valentines you leave around,
Signed: "Love from me, your favorite hound."

I do love you, you know, despite
The signature of doggy bite.
And I look forward to the days
You show your love in other ways.

HOUSE DOG SPEAKS

I'm a hearth dog,
   a heart dog,
   a hardy dog,
    a setter.

Show me one squirrel
   or one squab
   or one skunk —
    I'll get her.

I can roll in any,
   romp in any,
   run in any
    trash.

I can stumble into,
   tumble into,
   fumble into,
    S*P*L*A*S*H

Into icy lakes and
   blood-red steaks and
   cakes
    in nothing flat.

And there's not cat
   nor coon
   nor kid
    who's any good at that!

I AM DOG

I am tweed and carpet,
I am bark and bite,
I am red leaves falling,
I am morning's light,
I am banners waving,
I am moon of eye,
I am tongue's quick licking,
I am . . .
      I.

I am pounce of paw prints,
I am cooling nose,
I am water falling,
I am winter rose,
I am sandscape wriggle,
I am howl and cry,
I am stone and fortress,
I am . . .
      I.

To my friend Jane Yolen,
for helping me make my dream become real
— J. S.

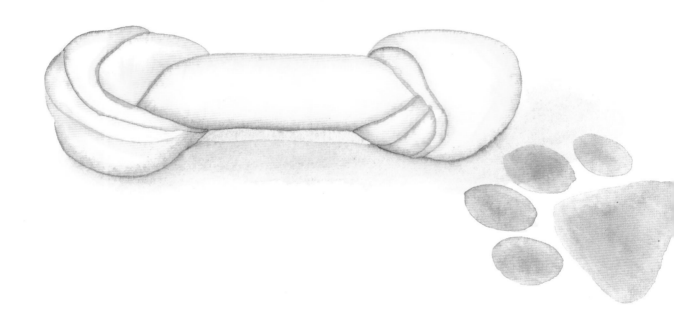

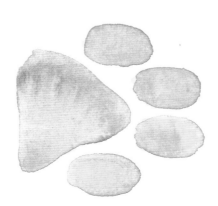